The Natural World

The Natural World

Brian Williams

Miles Kelly
PUBLISHING

Author
Brian Williams

Designed, Edited and Project Managed by
Starry Dog Books

Editor
Belinda Gallagher

Assistant Editor
Mark Darling

Artwork Commissioning
Lesley Cartlidge

Indexer
Janet De Saulles

Art Director
Clare Sleven

Editorial Director
Paula Borton

First published in 2001 by
Miles Kelly Publishing Ltd
The Bardfield Centre
Great Bardfield
Essex CM7 4SL

2468109753

Some material in this book can also be found in *The Greatest Book of the Biggest and Best*

Copyright © Miles Kelly Publishing Ltd 2001
This edition printed 2002

All rights reserved. No part of this publication may be reproduced,
stored in a retrieval system, or transmitted by any means, electronic, mechanical,
photocopying, recording or otherwise, without the prior permission of the
copyright holder.

A British Library Cataloguing-in-Publication Data.
A catalogue record for this book is available from the British Library

ISBN 1-84236-061-2
Printed in China

www.mileskelly.net
info@mileskelly.net

CONTENTS

LIVING THINGS	8
PLANTS AND FUNGI	10
TOWERING TREES	12
SLIDERS AND CRAWLERS	14
INTRIGUING INSECTS	16
FISH FACTS	18
AMPHIBIANS	20
REPTILES	22
BIRDS	24
MAMMALS	26
PREDATOR POWER	28
RECORD BREAKERS	30
DINOSAURS	32
EXTINCT AND VANISHING	34
THE NATURAL WORLD *QUIZ*	36
INDEX AND ACKNOWLEDGEMENTS	38

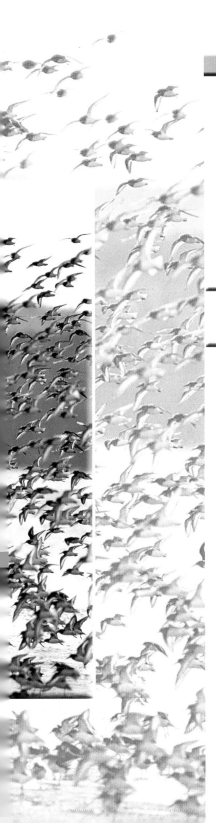

THE NATURAL

WORLD

The natural world surrounds us. Yet for most of the time we are not aware of the plant and animal kingdoms living, growing reproducing and changing right before our eyes.

From the minutest toadstool spores – up to five million are released in one go and carried by the wind – to enormous tree trunks – the sequoia measures more than 30 metres in diameter, the natural world provides us with amazing records and feats. For instance the common house spider can run at nearly 2 km per hour – that's the equivalent of a human being running 800 m in 10 seconds. Pretty fast. And parrots are so clever, they can work out simple sums.

Explore the biggest and best facts about *The Natural World* and get in touch with nature. There are the big, serious facts – for reference – and less serious ones, too, for fun. These pages are packed with the biggest and best, oddest and strangest, smallest and funniest facts around!

LIVING THINGS

Life on Earth began more than 3.5 billion years ago, when tiny cells divided and made copies of themselves. Scientists have named more than 2 million species of living things, and every year they find hundreds more new species. Living things range from microscopic bacteria to giant trees. Some live only for a day, others survive for thousands of years.

cell membran

cytoplasm

nucleus

▼ *There are two main groups of animals: vertebrates and invertebrates. Vertebrates are animals with backbones, such as a tiger. Invertebrates, such as a sea slug, do not have backbones. About 96 percent of all animals are invertebrates.*

▲ *All living things are made of cells. Cells are like tiny chemical factories. There are millions of them in our bodies. Different-shaped cells do different jobs. This is a typical animal cell.*

» BIGGEST GROUPS (NUMBERS OF SPECIES)

| Insects: 1 million plus | Plants: 375,000 | Arachnids: 110,000 (SPIDERS AND RELATIVES) | Roundworms: 100,000 (ESTIMATED) | Molluscs: 50,00 |

▶ *Insects are the biggest success story in the animal world. There are at least 1 million species.*

▶ *In this picture the size of each living thing is shown in proportion to how many species there are on Earth. There are at least 1 million insect species, so the ladybird is shown very big. But there are only 4,500 mammal species, so the elephant is tiny.*

mammal

OLDEST LIVING THINGS

	NAME	MILLION YEARS AGO
★ 1	Primitive algae and bacteria	3.5 billion years ago
2	Crustaceans	600
3	Molluscs	500
4	Fish	480
5	Land plants and millipedes	400
6	Insects and spiders	370
7	Amphibians	350
8	Reptiles	290
9	Mammals	190
10	Flowering plants	140

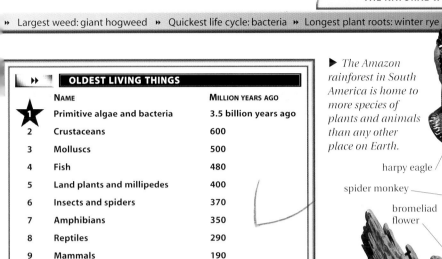

▶ *The Amazon rainforest in South America is home to more species of plants and animals than any other place on Earth.*

harpy eagle

spider monkey

bromeliad flower

◀ *Unlike plants, animals such as this mole must find their own food. Animals eat plants or other animals. For most animals, finding food is their main activity.*

anaconda

...hes: 27,000   Crustaceans: 26,000   Birds: 9,000   Reptiles: 5,000   Mammals: 4,500

blue-grey tanager

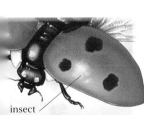

flaming poison arrow frog

bromeliad

insect

PLANTS AND FUNGI

There are about 375,000 species of plants. Some, such as mosses, ferns and lichens, never have flowers or make seeds. But most plants do make flowers – there are more than 250,000 flowering species. The earliest-known flowering plant grew 142 million years ago and a fossil of it was found in China in 1998. Plants make their own food, using sunlight, in a process called photosynthesis. Fungi are different from plants because they cannot make their own food. There are about 100,000 species of fungi.

poison ivy

nettle

water hemlock

saguaro cactus

◀ *The* Rafflesia *of Southeast Asia has the biggest flower, measuring 90 cm across. It also has a most disgusting smell, but flies love it!*

▲ *Plant defences discourage animals from eating them. Poison ivy gives off an oil that causes a painful itch. The hairs on nettle leaves cause a sting by injecting a fluid. The spines of cacti are too sharp to eat, and hemlock is so poisonous that animals eating its leaves or berries develop stomach ache and may even die.*

FUNGUS FEATS

● A single underground fungus mass beneath a forest in Washington state, USA, covers 6 sq km.

● A fungus mass in Michigan, USA, weighed more than 100 tonnes – as much as a blue whale.

➤➤ TALLEST, BIGGEST, LONGEST

Tallest grass	Bamboo	25 m
Tallest cactus	Saguaro	18 m
Biggest fern	Norfolk Island tree fern	20 m
Biggest seed	Coco-de-mer palm	20 kg
Biggest carnivorous	*Nepenthes* vines	10 m
Longest leaf	Raffia palm	20 m
	Amazonian bamboo palm	20 m
Longest seaweed	Giant kelp	60 m

◀ *The most deadly fungus is the death cap* Amanita phalloides. *If eaten, less than 50 g can kill a person in just six hours.*

Slowest flowering: *puya raimondii* ▸ Smallest: Brazilian duckweed ▸ Fastest growing: bamboo

IT'S A FACT

Some seeds can lie dormant for hundreds of years before they start to grow. In 1966 some frozen seeds of the Arctic lupin thawed and started to grow after they had been in deep freeze, scientists reckoned, for about 10,000 years.

▲ *Bamboo, a giant grass, is the fastest-growing plant. It shoots up almost 1 m a day.*

▲ *A Malaysian orchid has the longest petals, each one measuring almost 1 m long.*

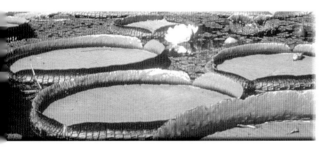

▲ *Measuring 2 m across, the leaves of the giant water-lily of tropical South America are so big and strong that a large frog can stand on them and walk across water!*

▼ *Toadstools, such as the ones shown here, are formed by a fungus when it is ready to reproduce. A single toadstool can contain 5 million tiny spores. These are released and blown away by the wind. When they land, they begin to grow into new fungi.*

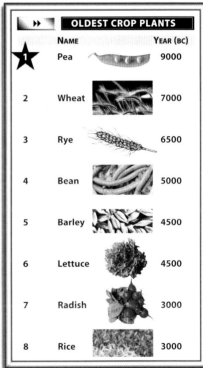

▸▸	OLDEST CROP PLANTS		
	NAME		**YEAR (BC)**
★ 1	Pea		9000
2	Wheat		7000
3	Rye		6500
4	Bean		5000
5	Barley		4500
6	Lettuce		4500
7	Radish		3000
8	Rice		3000

TOWERING TREES

Trees are the biggest plants, and the biggest single living thing on Earth is a tree. Trees live much longer than any animal. Some trees can survive for hundreds, and even thousands, of years. There are trees alive today that began growing long before the Roman Empire. Trees act as the Earth's 'lungs', enriching the air with oxygen. The trunks provide timber, and rubber is made from tree sap.

IT'S A FACT
The African baobab has a barrel-shaped trunk that stores water. The trunk can measure up to 54 m around the outside. Thirty people holding hands could just about make a circle around the trunk.

◀ *The banyan or Indian fig tree puts out wide-spreading branches that send down hundreds of hanging roots. These take hold of the soil and act as supports for the branches. The biggest-known banyan is in the Botanical Gardens in Calcutta, India. It has an estimated 1,775 hanging roots, and its huge canopy covers an area the size of a small forest.*

TREE SEEDS
● The fruits of the elm, ash, lime and hornbeam are fitted with aerofoils or wings that enable them to glide very long distances.
● The largest seed in the world comes from the giant fan palm or coco-de-mer, which grows only in the Seychelles. One seed can weigh 20 kg.
● Giant redwoods grow from tiny seeds less than 2 mm long.
● It would take 271,000 redwood seeds to make 1 kg!

SUPER GIANTS – THE TALLEST TREES EVER MEASURED

	NAME AND COUNTRY	HEIGHT
★1	Eucalyptus (Australia)	132.6 m
2	Douglas fir (USA)	126.5 m
3	Douglas fir (USA)	116 m
4	Mountain ash (Australia)	114 m
5	Coast redwood (USA)	112 m (STILL GROWING)

Greatest trunk girth: baobab » Heaviest: sequoia » Tallest ever: eucalyptus » Tallest and oldest living: redwood

The most massive tree is a giant sequoia named 'General Sherman' growing in Sequoia National Park, California, USA. This forest giant is almost 84 m high and measures 31.4 m round its trunk. It weighs an estimated 2,500 tonnes – as much as 350 elephants. Redwoods grow taller than giant sequoias, but their trunks are not as thick. They can reach heights of 100 m or more.

DID YOU KNOW?
The oldest living trees are bristlecone pines (left), in the USA, some of which are more than 4,000 years old. Giant sequoias probably have a lifespan of 5,000 to 6,000 years.

Counting tree leaves is not a job everyone would enjoy. The average oak grows and sheds at least 250,000 leaves every year.

SLIDERS AND CRAWLERS

The creepy crawlies of the animal world – insects, spiders, crustaceans, molluscs, worms, starfish and corals – are hugely varied, but they all have one thing in common: they lack backbones. They belong to the group called invertebrates. About 96 percent of all animals are invertebrates. The mollusc species alone number more than 100,000, and there are at least 1 million known insect species, though some scientists think there may be up to 10 million!

▶ *The house spider can run at nearly 2 km/h. Relative to its size, that is like a human sprinter running 800 m in 10 seconds – much faster than an Olympic athlete.*

◀ *The Gippsland giant worm is a 4-m-long Australian earthworm. It makes a slurping, gurgling sound as it slides its way through its burrow.*

▶ *The animals with the most legs are centipedes and millipedes. Millipedes, with up to 370 pairs, have the most, but centipedes can run faster.*

centipede

millipede

DID YOU KNOW?
The mantis shrimp can punch a hole in a glass tank. Called a stomatopod, this crustacean uses its spring-action smasher-claw to crack open crab shells and to hit other mantis shrimps in fights. Losers learn to back off when they meet a bigger rival, rather than risk being killed.

▶ *Some people keep African giant snails as pets. These leaf-munchers are the biggest land snails. The record-holder weighed 900 g and measured 39 cm across (as big as a football). Some sea snails are even bigger than the average African snail!*

The sea wasp jellyfish is the most venomous jellyfish. Its sting can kill a person in less than 4 minutes.

▶ *At 30 cm across, the robber crab is the biggest land crab. It can climb trees, and is so much a land animal that it drowns if kept in water.*

▸▸ LONGEST, BIGGEST, DEEPEST		
Longest worm	North sea bootlace worm	55 m
Biggest spider	Bird-eating spider	28 cm
Biggest sea snail	Horse conch	60 cm
Biggest starfish	*Midgardia xandaros*	1.38 m
Biggest jellyfish	Arctic giant jellyfish	body diameter: 2.28 m
		tentacle length: 36.5 m
Deepest-living sponge	*Hexactinellida* (class)	8,500 m

▼ *The giant squid is the largest-known invertebrate, measuring up to 6.1 m in body length, with tentacles up to 10.7 m long. Scientists believe these giants fight fierce battles with sperm whales, which hunt squid for food in the ocean depths.*

◀ *Pacific giant clams have the biggest shells of any mollusc. They can measure over 1 m across and weigh more than 300 kg. Clams grow very slowly – one tiny North Atlantic species takes 100 years to grow just 8 mm long.*

INTRIGUING INSECTS

Insects can live almost anywhere and eat almost anything. Fortunately their body design limits their size, so insect giants exist only in horror films! Many insects are amazingly strong. Some can drag objects many times heavier than themselves; others, such as termites, construct enormous homes; and fleas can jump 130 times their own height. Caterpillars may not look muscle-packed, but they have six times as many muscles as a person and they eat far more for their size.

BUTTERFLIES AND BEES

- A butterfly flaps its wings between 5 and 12 times per second.
- A queen bee lays 1 million eggs during her 5-year life.
- In spring a queen bee lays one egg every 40 seconds.

▶ *There are more beetles than any other kind of insect. The bombardier beetle has one of the most unusual weapons – it sprays a jet of hot, itch-making gas at attackers.*

IT'S A FACT
The fastest flyers in the insect world include dragonflies (left), which can reach speeds of up to 58 km/h. The bumblebee, by contrast, slowly buzzes along at less than half this speed – about 18 km/h.

▶ *The African Goliath beetle is the world's heaviest insect. It weighs about 100 g and at 11 cm long is almost as big as an adult person's hand.*

➤➤ NUMBERS OF INSECT SPECIES

Beetles: 400,000

Butterflies, moths: 165,000

Ants, bees, wasps: 140,000

Flies: 120,000

Bugs: 90,000

Locusts swarm in huge numbers. A small swarm may contain 50 million locusts. The largest-ever swarm, in Nebraska, USA, in 1875, had an estimated 12.5 million insects.

▸▸ INSECT RECORD-HOLDERS

Heaviest	Goliath beetle	100 g
Lightest	Bloodsucking banded louse (male)	0.005 mg
Longest legs	Stick insect	54.6 cm
Biggest mass	Locust swarm	25 million tonnes
Fastest runner	Tropical cockroach	5 km/h

Some locust species can eat their own body-weight in food every day.

Stick insects closely resemble twigs, making them hard for hungry birds to spot in the forests. The largest-known stick insect came from the rainforests of Borneo. It had a body length of 28 cm and its legs measured 54.6 cm – longer than a man's arm from elbow to fingertips!

▶ Termites make amazing mound nests. The tallest mound measured almost 9 m high. Termite queens live up to 50 years, making them the longest-lived insects.

FISH FACTS

Fish live in salty seas and freshwater rivers and lakes. Some are fast, streamlined swimmers, some have flat bodies and live on sea and river beds, some generate electricity, and some can even fly. Most fish have skeletons made of bone, but sharks have skeletons of cartilage. The biggest fish is the rare whale shark. The longest on record measured 12.6 m in length. This 15–20 tonne gentle giant eats only tiny plankton and small fish, but some of its relatives are among the most powerful predators in the world.

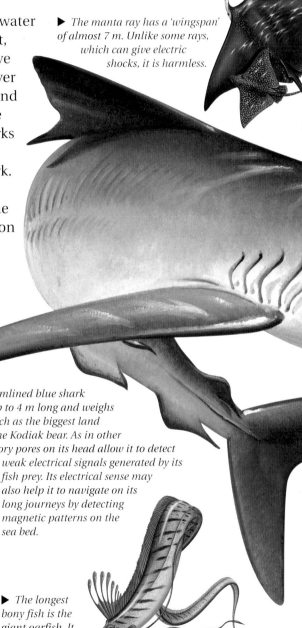

▶ *The manta ray has a 'wingspan' of almost 7 m. Unlike some rays, which can give electric shocks, it is harmless.*

▼ *The ocean sunfish, the heaviest bony fish, lays the most number of eggs at a single spawning – about 300 million. Only a tiny fraction of these develop. Most are eaten by other fish.*

▶ *The streamlined blue shark measures up to 4 m long and weighs twice as much as the biggest land carnivore, the Kodiak bear. As in other sharks, sensory pores on its head allow it to detect weak electrical signals generated by its fish prey. Its electrical sense may also help it to navigate on its long journeys by detecting magnetic patterns on the sea bed.*

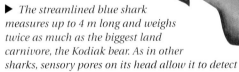

▶ *The longest bony fish is the giant oarfish. It is said to reach 15 m long.*

▼ *The 15-tonne whale shark, which lives in the warmer areas of the Atlantic, Pacific and Indian oceans, weighs almost as much as two big African bull elephants.*

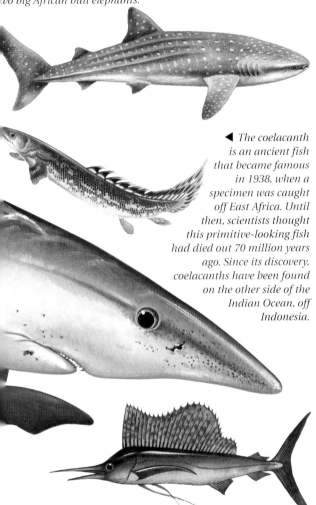

◀ *The coelacanth is an ancient fish that became famous in 1938, when a specimen was caught off East Africa. Until then, scientists thought this primitive-looking fish had died out 70 million years ago. Since its discovery, coelacanths have been found on the other side of the Indian Ocean, off Indonesia.*

The sailfish is the fastest swimmer, reaching just over 100 km/h in short bursts.

▸▸ BIGGEST FRESHWATER FISHES	
NAME	**LENGTH**
★ European giant catfish or wels	4.6 m
2 = Asian pla buk or pa beuk	3 m
2 = Sturgeon	3 m

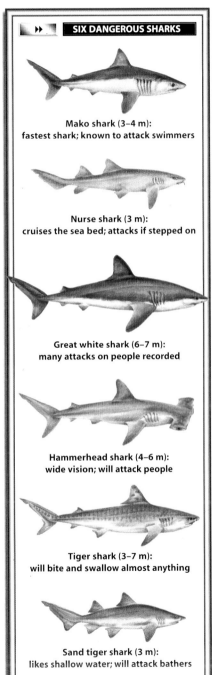

▸▸ SIX DANGEROUS SHARKS

Mako shark (3–4 m):
fastest shark; known to attack swimmers

Nurse shark (3 m):
cruises the sea bed; attacks if stepped on

Great white shark (6–7 m):
many attacks on people recorded

Hammerhead shark (4–6 m):
wide vision; will attack people

Tiger shark (3–7 m):
will bite and swallow almost anything

Sand tiger shark (3 m):
likes shallow water; will attack bathers

AMPHIBIANS

There are about 3,000 species of amphibians altogether. Most of them – about 2,700 – are frogs and toads, which have no tails. Frogs hunt by shooting out their long, sticky-tipped tongues to grab insects. The largest of this group is the African Goliath frog. The second-biggest group is the newts and salamanders, which do have tails. The members of the smallest group are called caecilians. They have no legs and look like worms. All amphibians are cold-blooded animals and most can live on land or in water.

FROG FACTS AND FEATS

- Some frogs hardly ever leave the water.
- Some frogs burrow in the ground.
- Some frogs climb trees using sucker discs on their toes.
- There is even a gliding frog, which leaps between branches.

▼ *The Pacific giant salamander is the largest of the salamanders in northwestern North America. It grows to 28 cm long.*

FATTEST, BIGGEST, SMALLEST		
Fattest toad:	Cane toad	2.6 kg
Biggest amphibian:	Chinese giant salamander	1.8 m
Biggest frog:	African Goliath frog	3.6 kg
Biggest tadpole:	Mexican axolotl	25 cm
Smallest frog:	*Eleutherodactylus limbatus*	12 mm

▶ *A frog jumps by lifting its front legs off the ground and pushing off with its strong back legs. Almost any frog can leap 20 times its own length. The record jump is 10.3 m by a pet South African sharp-nosed frog.*

▶ *The red eyed tree frog of Central America lives on the underside of leaves in lowland rainforests. The distinctive vertical black pupils in the frog's eyes, like those of a cat, give it excellent night vision. Frogs generally have horizontal pupils for daylight vision.*

Loudest: bullfrog » Oddest: axolotl » Smallest: Cuban micro-frog *Eleutherodactylus limbatus*

The frogs of today are descended from much larger creatures that first crept onto land around 300 million years ago. Like the first amphibians, they have to return to water to reproduce.

The oddest amphibian is the Mexican axolotl, a salamander that never completes its metamorphosis from tadpole to an adult. It remains a giant tadpolelike creature all its life, breathing through gills. The axolotl can never leave the water to explore dry land.

▼ *The cane toad is the greatest amphibian pest. It was introduced to Australia from tropical South America in the 1930s to eat beetles. Unfortunately it also gobbles up native frogs and lizards, and even birds. The largest known was 53.9 cm long.*

◀ *The California newt of the United States is about 15 cm long, just smaller than Europe's biggest newt, the warty newt. Newts are salamanders that spend most of their adult lives in water.*

Amphibians have some strange names. The mudpuppy, shown here, is a salamander. Perhaps more oddly named still is the stumpy rocketfrog, which lives in Australia.

DID YOU KNOW?
In British English frogs go "croak". In American English they go "ribbit". Korean frogs say "gae-gool, gae-gool", and Russian frogs go "kva-kva".

REPTILES

There are about 3,700 species of lizards, making this the biggest group of reptiles. The next largest group is snakes. But the biggest living reptile is neither a lizard nor a snake. It is the estuarine or saltwater crocodile, which can be up to 7 m long. The largest crocodiles weigh as much as 450 kg and can live to be 100 years old. Only a leatherback turtle outweighs a crocodile. One specimen that washed up on a beach in Wales, UK, in 1988 weighed more than 960 kg. The heaviest snake is the anaconda at 200 kg.

DID YOU KNOW?

There are only two poisonous lizards, the Mexican beaded lizard and the gila monster (right) of the southwestern United States. The gila monster's favourite food is birds' eggs. It bites humans only in self-defence. Its brittle teeth may remain in the wound.

▼ *The leatherback turtle is the heaviest reptile and also one of the fastest, reaching speeds of 35 km/h when scared.*

▼ *One of the most venomous snakes is the king cobra. It is also the longest poisonous snake. It can grow to more than 4.5 m long.*

hawksbi

loggerhead turtle

gree turtle

leatherback turtle

DEADLY SNAKES

● Without treatment, victims of the taipan, black mamba, tiger snake, common krait and king cobra have a 50 to 100 percent risk of dying.

● Sea snakes in the Timor Sea have venom 100 times stronger than the taipan's.

▼ *The Komodo dragon, an Indonesian monitor lizard, can grow to 3 m in length. Animals three times this size have been reported, but not proved.) Komodos use their sawlike teeth to tear meat from their prey, which includes water buffaloes. Human victims have also been reported.*

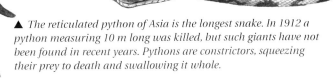

▲ *The reticulated python of Asia is the longest snake. In 1912 a python measuring 10 m long was killed, but such giants have not been found in recent years. Pythons are constrictors, squeezing their prey to death and swallowing it whole.*

»	BIGGEST CROCODILES AND ALLIGATORS	
	NAME	**LENGTH**
★ 1	Estuarine crocodile	7 m
2	Indian gavial	6 m
3 =	Nile crocodile	5 m
3 =	American crocodile	5 m
4	American alligator	4 m

◀ *Geckos have an unusual adaptation – hairy feet. Each foot has about 500,000 hairs, and each hair tip has thousands of microscopic 'stickers', creating a powerful adhesive. This enables the gecko to walk on any surface and even hang by one toe.*

▲ *The estuarine crocodile often swims far out in the Indian Ocean. At up to 7 m long, it is the biggest of all the crocodiles.*

BIRDS

Birds are the only animals with feathers and they all have wings, though not all of them can fly. Among the biggest expert flyers are the storks, condors, swans and albatrosses. Record-breaking flyers are the peregrine falcon, the fastest of all birds, and the Arctic tern, which makes the longest migratory flight of any bird, from the Arctic to Antarctica and back again. The ostrich is the biggest living bird, but it is flightless. It can run at speeds of up to 50 km/h.

▲ *The wandering albatross glides effortlessly across thousands of kilometres of ocean. It has the longest wing-span of any living bird, measuring up to 3.6 m.*

»	LONGEST-LIVED BIRDS	
	NAME	**AGE (YEARS)**
1	Siberian white crane	82
2 =	Sulphur-crested cockatoo	80
2 =	Goose	80
3 =	Ostrich	68
3 =	Eagle owl	68
4	Macaw	64

▶ *With their long necks and stilt-like legs, flamingos stand up to 1.5 m tall. They live in lakes and marshland in eastern and southern Africa, and use their curved bills to catch small water creatures. Parent birds feed their single chick on liquidized babyfood from their stomachs.*

IT'S A FACT
Birds' feathers are light, waterproof and provide insulation, slowing down heat loss. A swan (left) has about 25,000 feathers. Hummingbirds have the fewest: less than 1,000. Their feathers resemble scales.

◀ *In a dive a peregrine falcon can reach an estimated speed of 270 km/h, making it the fastest of all creatures. It knocks its prey out of the air, killing it instantly.*

▶ *Bird-brains are quite bright. Ravens and pigeons can work out simple counting sums. Parrots (right) and mynahs can mimic human speech, and some parrots can name and count objects.*

▸▸ BIGGEST EAGLES	
NAME	**LENGTH**
★1 Harpy eagle (South America)	100 cm
2 = Monkey-eating eagle (Philippines)	90 cm
2 = Crowned eagle (Africa)	90 cm
2 = Steller's sea eagle (Pacific coasts)	90 cm

◀ *The bald eagle is the national bird of the United States. Its huge nest can be up to 2.9 m wide and 6 m deep.*

◀ *The ostrich can be as tall as 2.7 m and weigh more than 150 kg. It lays the biggest of all birds' eggs. At up to 20 cm long, one egg would make about 12 omelettes!*

▶ *The 10.2-cm-long beak of the sword-billed hummingbird is longer than its body, making it the longest beak in relation to body length.*

▼ *The lesser flamingo of eastern Africa lives in huge flocks that can number several million birds.*

▸▸ LONGEST WING-SPANS	
NAME	**LENGTH**
★1 Wandering albatross	3.6 m
2 Marabou stork	3.2 m
3 = Andean condor	3 m
3 = Swan	3 m

MAMMALS

The biggest animals in the world on land and in the sea are both mammals: elephants and whales. Amazingly adaptable, mammals live in a diverse range of habitats from desert and rainforests to mountains, caves and ocean depths. They have bigger brains in relation to their body size than other animals. Many have hair or fur and some have scales or spines. But all mammals have one thing in common: they suckle their young with milk.

▸▸ HEAVIEST HOOFED MAMMALS		
NAME	**WEIGHT**	**HEIGHT**
★1 White rhinoceros	3,000 kg	1.8 m
2 Hippopotamus	1,400 kg	1.5 m
3 Giraffe	1,200 kg	5.5 m
4 = Shire horse	1,000 kg	1.7 m
4 = American bison	1,000 kg	1.5 m

▼ *There are about 4,500 mammal species ranging in size from the giant blue whale at 33.5 m long to tiny shrews and bats. Shown here to scale, the blue whale dwarfs the biggest land mammals and a human.*

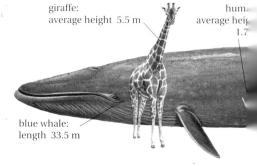

giraffe: average height 5.5 m

human: average height 1.7

◀ *The biggest land animal is the African elephant. A big bull from the grasslands often weighs more than 6 tonnes. Forest elephants are usually smaller.*

blue whale: length 33.5 m

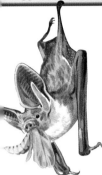

◀ *Bats are the only true flying mammals. In size they range from tiny bats no bigger than a bumblebee to flying foxes, which are as big as guinea pigs with wing-spans of 1.5 m. The small insect-eating bats, such as this long-eared bat, hunt by night using high-frequency echolocation. This means they collect sound reflections in their ear flaps.*

The blue whale is the biggest of all the mammals and gives birth to the biggest baby. At birth, a blue whale calf already measures 6 to 8 m long.

▲ *The elk, or moose, is the biggest of all the deer, weighing 800 kg. Its antlers can be up to 1.5 m across. An elk eats the equivalent of about 20,000 leaves a day.*

▶ *The giraffe is the tallest mammal and has the longest neck. At full stretch a full-grown giraffe can reach juicy leaves up to 6 m above the ground.*

↠	LARGEST WHALES	
	NAME	**LENGTH**
★ 1	Blue whale	33.5 m
2	Fin whale	25 m
3 =	Sei whale (shown), Humpback whale	19 m
4	Sperm whale	18.5 m

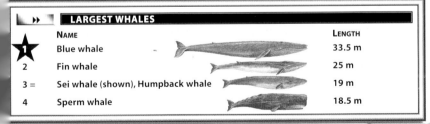

Brown bear: average height 2.4 m

African elephant: average height 3.3 m

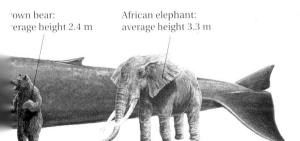

SLOW SLOTH

● The sloth is the slowest mammal. It crawls at 2 m a minute on the ground, speeding up to twice that when hanging upside-down from a tree.

PREDATOR POWER

The carnivores, or meat-eaters, include some of the most powerful predators in the animal world. The most feared hunters of the ocean are the great sharks and the killer whale, which can tackle even the biggest male seals and sea lions. The biggest land carnivores are the bears and the big cats. But smaller predators also show great determination and strength when hunting.

CATS ON THE PROWL

- Tigers hunt alone.
- Lions hunt in groups, driving prey into ambush.
- Jaguars often hunt in water.
- Leopards climb trees.
- Cheetahs chase prey at high speed.

▼ *The biggest bears in the world are the polar bear and the brown Kodiak bear (shown here) of Kodiak Island off Alaska. These huge North American bears can stand 3 m tall on their hind legs and weigh about 750 kg.*

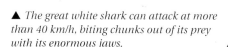

▲ *The great white shark can attack at more than 40 km/h, biting chunks out of its prey with its enormous jaws.*

► *Killer whales hunt in groups called pods. They will pursue fleeing seals into the shallows and even charge through the surf to grab seals from the beach.*

 TOP PREDATORS IN THE SEA AND ON LAND

Killer whale:
9 m; 9,000 kg

Great white shark:
4.5 m; 3,300 kg

Elephant seal:
5 m; 2,300 kg

Estuarine crocodile:
7 m; 450 kg

Steller's sea lion
3.3 m; 1,000 kg

▲ *Wolves (above) and African hunting dogs hunt in packs, chasing bigger animals such as deer or antelope until the prey is exhausted and can be killed.*

▲ *The male Siberian tiger is the biggest of the big cats, measuring 3.2 m from nose to tail tip. It is the most northern species of tiger, and is at home in the snow. Only about 400 are alive in the wild today.*

e: This list does not include other sharks and marine mammals, which are bigger than the biggest land predators

| Kodiak bear: | Polar bear: | Grizzly bear: | Siberian tiger: | Lion: |
| 3 m; 750 kg | 2.6 m; 900 kg | 2.5 m; 400 kg | 3.2 m; 300 kg | 3 m; 250 kg |

RECORD BREAKERS

The record-breakers of the natural world come in all shapes and sizes. Many animals are unbelievably strong. Some insects and mammals have incredible appetites. The fastest animals can easily outstrip a human sprinter, and the noisiest can outshout the loudest soccer fans. But for sheer size, the prize goes to the majestic blue whale. No creature in the history of the Earth has been bigger than this giant of the oceans. It eats only tiny, shrimplike krill, but swallows millions in one mouthful.

◄ *The noisiest land animals are the red and black howler monkeys of South America, the biggest of the New World monkeys. Living in troops of 10 to 30 animals, the monkeys howl to define their territory. The sound is made louder by the echo chambers beneath their chins, and can be heard 5 km away.*

IT'S A FACT
Some caterpillars eat more than 100 times their own weight of food every day during the first 8 weeks of life. Shrews also have huge appetites and eat nearly all the time.

▶ *The sperm whale is the biggest toothed whale, reaching 18 m in length and weighing 70 t. It dives to great depths, plunging to 3,000 m to hunt for food.*

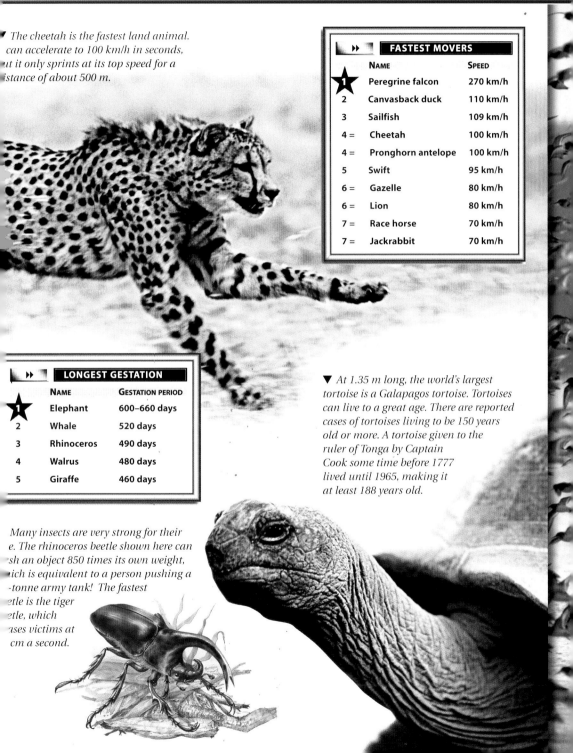

The cheetah is the fastest land animal. *can accelerate to 100 km/h in seconds,* *ut it only sprints at its top speed for a* *istance of about 500 m.*

FASTEST MOVERS		
	NAME	**SPEED**
1	Peregrine falcon	270 km/h
2	Canvasback duck	110 km/h
3	Sailfish	109 km/h
4 =	Cheetah	100 km/h
4 =	Pronghorn antelope	100 km/h
5	Swift	95 km/h
6 =	Gazelle	80 km/h
6 =	Lion	80 km/h
7 =	Race horse	70 km/h
7 =	Jackrabbit	70 km/h

LONGEST GESTATION		
	NAME	**GESTATION PERIOD**
1	Elephant	600–660 days
2	Whale	520 days
3	Rhinoceros	490 days
4	Walrus	480 days
5	Giraffe	460 days

▼ *At 1.35 m long, the world's largest tortoise is a Galapagos tortoise. Tortoises can live to a great age. There are reported cases of tortoises living to be 150 years old or more. A tortoise given to the ruler of Tonga by Captain Cook some time before 1777 lived until 1965, making it at least 188 years old.*

Many insects are very strong for their *e. The rhinoceros beetle shown here can* *sh an object 850 times its own weight,* *ich is equivalent to a person pushing a* *-tonne army tank! The fastest* *etle is the tiger* *etle, which* *ases victims at* *cm a second.*

DINOSAURS

For about 160 million years, from 225 million years ago to 65 million years ago, dinosaurs were the most successful animals on Earth. The giant dinosaurs were the biggest reptiles of all time, and some of the prehistoric reptiles were the biggest flying animals ever. The word dinosaur means 'terrible lizard', and the names of the different dinosaurs describe something about them. *Tyrannosaurus*, for example, means 'tyrant lizard'.

▼ *Among the most fearsome dinosaurs were the 'slashing-claw' hunters such as the 4-m-long* Deinonychus, *the human-sized* Velociraptor *and the smaller* Stenonychosaurus. *These species were probably among the most intelligent too.*

Deinonychus

Velociraptor

Stenonychosaurus

▸ SOME ARMOURED GIANTS

1 *Ankylosaurus:* 10 m long

2 *Triceratops:* 9 m long

3 *Stegosaurus:* 7 m long

▸ SOME DINOSAUR GIANTS			Note: This list is a selection of some of the biggest dinosa
NAME	**LENGTH**	**WEIGHT**	
1 *Seismosaurus*	30–50 m	50–80 tonnes	
2 *Brachiosaurus*	25 m	50 tonnes	
3 *Diplodocus*	23–27 m	12 tonnes	
4 *Mamenchisaurus*	20 m	uncertain	
5 *Apatosaurus (Brontosaurus)*	20 m	20–30 tonnes	1

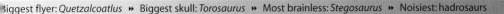
Biggest flyer: *Quetzalcoatlus* » Biggest skull: *Torosaurus* » Most brainless: *Stegosaurus* » Noisiest: hadrosaurs

Pterosaurs lived at same time as dinosaurs and were related, were not dinosaurs themselves. They flew wings of skin. The largest, with a wing- n of 15 m, was Quetzalcoatlus. It was as as a small aeroplane.

▲ The loudest dinosaurs were probably the duck-billed hadrosaurs. Like blowing trumpets, they blew air through cavities in their bony heads to make bellowing calls.

◄ The most terrifying carnivorous dinosaurs were Tyrannosaurus Rex (shown here) and the earlier Allosaurus. These hunters were up to 12 m long, weighed 6 tonnes, and had enormous jaws lined with sharp teeth.

DID YOU KNOW?
Why the dinosaurs died out remains a mystery. The likeliest explanation is that a comet or meteorite hit the Earth, sending up huge dust-clouds on impact that caused a climate change. This killed off the plants on which many dinosaurs fed, and may have affected the hatching of dinosaur eggs.

EXTINCT AND VANISHING

Thousands of animals have died out naturally during the course of evolution. Most extinctions happen when animals cannot adapt to changes in the environment. Several mass extinctions happened in prehistoric times. The largest took place 240 million years ago, when perhaps 96 percent of living things vanished. The best-known mass extinction, 65 million years ago, saw the disappearance of the dinosaurs. Extinctions have greatly increased in the last 200 years, because of human activities.

»»	BIGGEST PREHISTORIC AN
Baluchitherium	Giant rhinocero
Megatherium	Ground sloth
Glyptodon	Armadillo
Diprotodon	Giant Australia
Diatryma	Carnivorous bir

◀ *The dodo lived undisturbed on the island of Mauritius in the Indian Ocean until European sailors arrived in the 1500s. Sailors killed the birds for food and rats and cats ate the eggs. By 1680 the dodo was extinct.*

Baluchitherium

giant moa

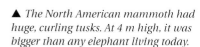

▲ *The North American mammoth had huge, curling tusks. At 4 m high, it was bigger than any elephant living today.*

◀ *Baluchitherium was bigger than any land mammal alive today, and the gian moa was taller than any living bird. A human would be dwarfed by these gian*

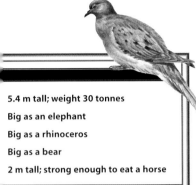

5.4 m tall; weight 30 tonnes

Big as an elephant

Big as a rhinoceros

Big as a bear

2 m tall; strong enough to eat a horse

◄ *Billions of passenger pigeons lived in North America during the 19th century. But hunters began killing them in their breeding colonies, and between 1850 and 1880 the pigeon flocks vanished. The last passenger pigeon died in a zoo in 1914.*

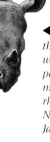

◄ *Big cats are becoming rare as humans encroach on their hunting grounds. Among the rarest is the snow leopard of western China. It has a territory of up to 100 sq km.*

GONE FOREVER

● Steller's sea cow, a giant sea mammal, weighed 10 tonnes.
● The giant Irish deer had antlers with a span of 4 m.

◄ *Hunted for their horns, which some people value as a medicine, all the world's rhinoceroses are endangered. No more than 50 one-horned Javan rhinos are left in the wild.*

▼ *The North American buffalo, or bison, had a narrow escape. Two hundred years ago millions of buffalo wandered the Great Plains, but hunters in the 1800s killed most of them and by 1881 only 551 were left. Now protected, numbers have increased and there are more than 30,000 in the United States and Canada.*

RARE EUROPEAN BROWN BEARS

European brown bears are among the rarest animals, with only scattered populations.

COUNTRY	POPULATION
1 France (Pyrenees)	10
2 Austria	30
3 Italy	80
4 Spain	85
5 Greece	120

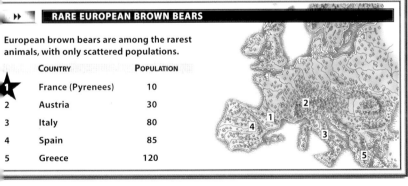

7. Beetles » 8. Ostrich » 9. Peregrine falcon » 10. Blue whale » 11. Kodiak Island, off Alaska » 12. Caterpillar
18. Seismosaurus » 19. Quetzalcoatlus » 20. Hadrosaurs

THE NATURAL WORLD *QUIZ*

Now that you have read all about what's biggest and best in The Natural World, see if you can answer these 20 quiz questions! (Pictures give clues, answers at the top of the page.)

▶ 4. What living giant has the nickname 'General Sherman'?

▶ 2. What kind of grass grows higher than a house?

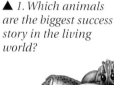
▲ 3. Which tree has over 1,700 hanging roots?

▲ 1. Which animals are the biggest success story in the living world?

▼ 6. Which has the most legs – a centipede or a millipede?

▲ 5. Can robber crabs drown?

▶ 7. Which are most numerous – beetles or flies?

▶ 8. Which bird can grow up to 2.7 m tall?

▶ 9. Which is the fastest bird?

▼ 10. Which is the biggest mammal?

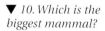

▼ 13. Which are the biggest big cats?

▲ 12. Which creature can eat more than 100 times its own weight in a day?

▲ 11. Where do the biggest bears live?

▼ 14. Which land animals make the most noise?

▲ 15. Which fish is the fastest swimmer?

▼ 16. Which insect can pull 850 times its own weight?

▲ 17. What was the biggest mammal ever to walk on land?

◄ 18. Which was the heaviest dinosaur?

► 20. Which were the loudest dinosaurs?

▲ 19. Which pterosaur was as big as a plane?

INDEX

Entries in bold refer to
illustrations

A
Africa 19, 24, 25, 29
algae 9
alligator 23
amphibian 9, **20-21**
animal **8**, **9**, 10, **14-35**
Antarctica 8, 24
antelope 29, 31
arachnid 8
Arctic 24
Asia 10, 23
Australia 21
Austria 35
axolotl **21**

B
bacteria 8, 9
Baluchitherium **34**
bamboo **11**
banyan 12
baobab **12**
bat 26, 27
bear 18, 27, **28**, **29**, 35
  brown **27**
  grizzly **29**
  kodiak **28**, 29
  polar **29**
bee 16, 27
beetle 16, 30, **31**
bird **24-25**, 34, 35
  bald eagle **25**
  blue-grey tanager **9**
  dodo **34**
  duck 31
  flamingo **24**
  giant moa **34**

harpy eagle **9**
hummingbird **25**
ostrich **25**
parrot **25**
passenger pigeon **35**
penguin 25
peregrine falcon **25**, 31
pigeon 35
raven 35
swan **24**
swift 31
  wandering albatross 35
bristlecone pine **13**
buffalo 23, **34-35**
bug **16**
butterfly **8**, **16**

C
cactus **10**
caecilian 20
Canada 35
carnivore 28
caterpillar **30**, 31
cave 26
cell **8**
centipede **14**
Central America 20
cheetah, 27, 28, **30-31**
China 10, 35
clam **15**
coelacanth 19
coral 14
crab **15**
crocodile 22, **23**, **28**
crustacean **9**, 14

D
deer 27, 29, 35
defences 10
desert 26
dinosaur **32-33**, 34
dog 11
dragonfly **16**

E
egg 16, 18, 22, 25, 33, 34, 35
elephant **8**, 13, 19, **26**, **27**, 31, 34
environment 34
evolution 34
extinction **34-35**

F
fish **9**, **18-19**
  coelacanth **19**
  giant oarfish **18**
  manta ray **18**
  ocean sunfish **18**
  sailfish **19**
flower **9**, **10**
fly **16**,
food 9, 10, 15, 17, 30, 34
France 35
frog **9**, **20-21**
fruit 12
fungi **10-11**

G
gas 16
giant sequoia **13**
giant water-lily **11**
giraffe **26**, **27**, 31
Greece 35

H
habitat 26
horse 31
human 26

I
Indonesia 19
insect **8**, **9**, 14, **16-17**, 20, 30, 31
invertebrate 8, 14, 15
Italy 35

J
jaguar 28
jellyfish **15**

K/L

krill 30, 31
ladybird 8, **9**
leaf **11**, **13**
leopard 28, **35**
lion 28, **29**, 31
lizard 22, 23
    gecko **22-23**
    gila monster 22, **23**
    komodo dragon 23
    mexican beaded 22
locust **17**

M

mammal 8, **9**, **26-7**, 30, **34**, 35
mantis shrimp **14**
millipede **14**
mole **9**
mollusc 8, 9, 14, **15**
monkey **9**, 30
moose 27
mountain 26
mudpuppy **21**

N

nest **17**, 25
nettle **10**
newt 20, **21**
North America 20, 35

O

oak **13**
ocean 19, 23, 24, 26, 28, 30, 34
octopus 14
orchid **11**

P

photosynthesis 10
plankton 18
plant 8, 9, **10-11**, **12-13**, 33
poison ivy **10**
predator 18, **28-29**
prey 23, 25, 29

R

rafflesia **10**
rainforest 9, 17, 26
reptile 9, **22-23**, **32-33**
rhinoceros 26, 31, **35**

S

salamander **20**, **21**
scorpion 15
sea cow 35
sea lion **28**
seal **28**
shark **18-19**
    blue **18**
    great white **19**, 28
    hammerhead **19**
    mako **19**
    nurse **19**
    sand tiger **19**
    tiger **19**
    whale **19**
skeleton 18
sloth 27
slug **8**
snail 14, 15
snake 9, 22
    black mamba 22
    common krait 22
    king cobra **22**
    python 22
    reticulated python **23**
    sea 22
    taipan 22
    tiger 22
snow leopard **35**
South America 9, 11, 21, 30
Spain 35
species 8, 9, 10, 14, 20, 22, 29
spider 9, **14**, 15
    house **14**
squid **15**
starfish 14, 15
stick insect **17**

T

termite 17
tiger 8, 28, **29**
toad 20, **21**
tortoise **31**
tree 8, **12-13**, 15, 20, 27
turtle **22**

U/V

UK 22
USA 10, 17, 21, 22, 25, 35
vertebrate 8

W

walrus 31
water 18, 20, 21
water hemlock **10**
whale 8, **15**, **26-27**, **28**, **30**, 31
    killer **28**
    sperm **15**, 30
wind 11
wolf **29**
wooly mammoth **34**
worm 8, **14**, 15
    Gippsland giant worm **14**
    roundworm **8**

*The publishers wish to thank the following artists
who have contributed to this book:*

Jim Channell, John Francis, Rob Jakeway, Stuart Lafford, Mick Loates,
Alan Male, Janos Marffy, Terry Riley, Martin Sanders, Mike Saunders,
Rudi Vizi, Christian Webb

*The publishers wish to thank the following sources
for the photographs used in this book:*

CORBIS: Page 10 (C/L) John Holmes; Frank Lane Picture Agency;
Page 17 (T/L) Philip Richardson; Gallo Images; Page 18 (B/L)
Philip Richardson; Gallo Images; Page 23 (B/R) Paul A. Souders;
Page 28 (B/R) Paul A. Souders
All other photographs from Miles Kelly Archives